# Contents

Words in **bold** are in the glossary.

# Robo-warriors and the natural world

An unmanned aircraft called the MQ-9 Reaper streaked across the sky like an attacking eagle. The target was the **terrorist** group ISIS. The United States military battled this group in 2016. Enemy fighters tested the soldiers' skills. The armed forces fought back with unmanned aircraft. The Reaper and the MQ-1 Predator made many perfect strikes. They caused little damage and spared innocent lives.

The MQ-1 and MQ-9 used special sensors. They worked like some animals' eyes. Some snakes, frogs and fish can see **infrared** light. Animals use this light to help locate prey. The MQ-1 also used it to locate targets.

infrared image

# BEASTLY ROBOTS AND DRONES

## MILITARY TECHNOLOGY INSPIRED BY ANIMALS

Lisa M. Bolt Simons

Raintree is an imprint of Capstone Global Library Limited, a company incorporated in England and Wales having its registered office at 264 Banbury Road, Oxford, OX2 7DY – Registered company number: 6695582

www.raintree.co.uk
myorders@raintree.co.uk

Edited by Aaron Sautter
Designed by Kyle Grenz
Original illustrations © Capstone Global Library Limited 2021
Picture research by Morgan Walters
Production by Katy LaVigne
Originated by Capstone Global Library Ltd
Printed and bound in India

978 1 4747 9386 5 (hardback)
978 1 4747 9394 0 (paperback)

**British Library Cataloguing in Publication Data**
A full catalogue record for this book is available from the British Library.

**Acknowledgements**
We would like to thank the following for permission to reproduce photographs: Alamy: AB Forces News Collection, bottom 15, 615 collection, 18, Aviation History Collection, top left 13, CPC Collection, top 19, Niday Picture Library, bottom 9, PJF Military Collection, top 7, bottom 20, Science History Images, bottom 26; Associated Press: Christof Stache, bottom 7; Getty Images: John B. Carnett, 22; iStockphoto: danku, (plane) 16-17; Newscom: Dean Murray/DARPA/Cover Images, top 24, Rodrigo Reyes Marin/AFLO, 29; Shutterstock: aapsky, middle 5, Alexia Khruscheva, top 21, Artistdesign29, design element throughout, Bravo_Roger, (hand) left 20, Cathy Keifer, top 9, clarst5, left 16, Creeping Things, (lizard) 10, DarkGeometryStudios, top 28, Dennis Jacobsen, top right 25, Eric Isselee, (skunk) bottom left 25, GJGK Photography, 12, Image Point Fr, 4, In Green, 6, KN2018, top 26, Mark Medcalf, top 15, Martin Mecnarowski, (bird) 17, Martin Voeller, bottom 24, Mirek Kijewski, 23, Nayana Willemyns, bottom 21, Ociacia, bottom 28, Omelchenko, design element throughout, Phillip Rubino, top 5, photosounds, (cat) Cover, reptiles4all, bottom 5, sandyman, (robot) Cover, seeyou, 27, Seregraff, (cat) bottom 13, Suzanne Tucker, bottom 19, Ultraviolet_Photographer, 14; Wikimedia: Denniss, 11, Marshall Astor, middle right 13.

Every effort has been made to contact copyright holders of material reproduced in this book. Any omissions will be rectified in subsequent printings if notice is given to the publisher.

All the internet addresses (URLs) given in this book were valid at the time of going to press. However, due to the dynamic nature of the internet, some addresses may have changed, or sites may have changed or ceased to exist since publication. While the author and publisher regret any inconvenience this may cause readers, no responsibility for any such changes can be accepted by either the author or the publisher.

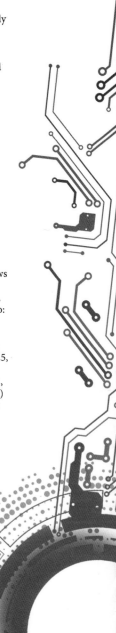

MQ-9 Reapers soar on wide wings and spot distant targets just like eagles.

Both snakes and MQ-9s use infrared light to find targets.

## Imitating nature

Military ground robots are called unmanned ground vehicles (UGVs). Like mules or horses, these robots carry supplies on the battlefield. They also carry injured soldiers to safety.

Many robots and drones are designed to imitate animals. This process is called **biomimicry**. *Bio* means "life". *Mimesis* means "to imitate". Drones and robots often do dangerous jobs that humans can't. Some experts believe these machines are the future of the military. By 2025 or 2030, robots may outnumber troops in combat.

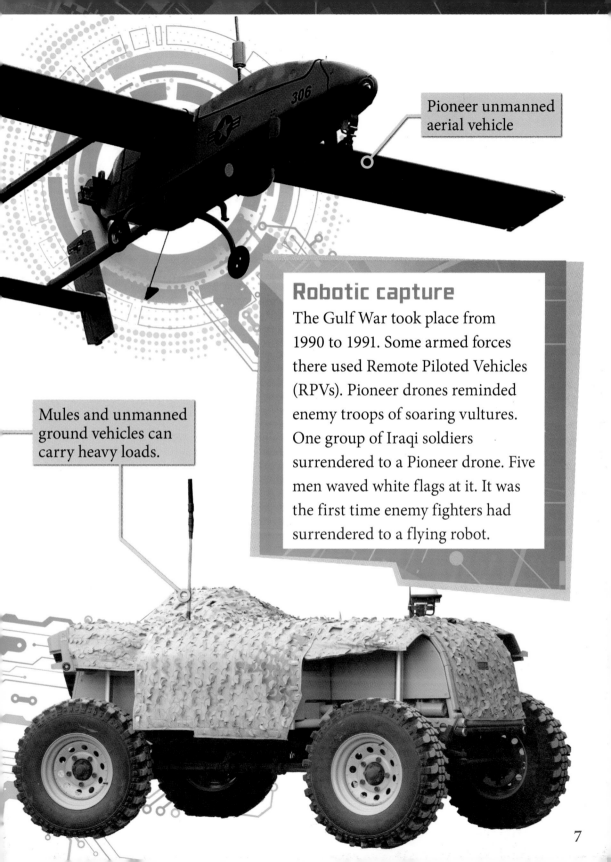

Pioneer unmanned aerial vehicle

Mules and unmanned ground vehicles can carry heavy loads.

## Robotic capture

The Gulf War took place from 1990 to 1991. Some armed forces there used Remote Piloted Vehicles (RPVs). Pioneer drones reminded enemy troops of soaring vultures. One group of Iraqi soldiers surrendered to a Pioneer drone. Five men waved white flags at it. It was the first time enemy fighters had surrendered to a flying robot.

# Past inventions lead to a robotic future

The natural world is dangerous. Animals have abilities that help them to survive. Battlefields are also deadly. To keep soldiers safe, researchers often look to nature. They create machines that imitate animal features.

Armies began building unmanned vehicles in World War I (1914–1918). French forces created the Crocodile Schneider. This small tracked machine crawled like a crocodile. It blew up when it reached its target.

US armed forces tried making unmanned **aerial** vehicles (UAVs) too. The Kettering Bug was like a **torpedo** with wings. After a set amount of time, the engine shut off. The craft would then drop like a bomb to hit its target. But the war ended before the Bug was ready for combat.

The Kettering Bug flew like a fluttering moth or butterfly.

# Natural defences

Skunks and stink bugs can spray chemicals from their bodies. The short-horned lizard can squirt blood from its eyes! Animals use this ability for self-defence. Armies found this feature useful too.

In World War II (1939–1945) the Soviet Union invented the Teletank. Like some animals, the remote-controlled tank could spray enemies. It could shoot smoke, fire or chemicals.

skunk

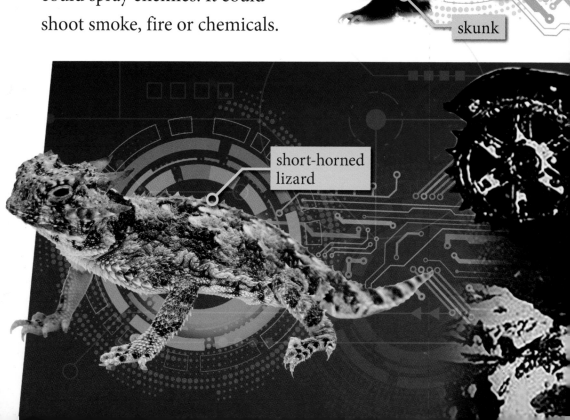

short-horned lizard

Some machines were designed to make surprise attacks. The US Navy created the Salamander in 1944. The unmanned craft crawled from the water to blow up enemy defences. Like real salamanders, it could travel both in the water and on land.

Soviet TT-26 remotely controlled Teletank

## Eyes and ears in Vietnam

Drones were important in the Vietnam War (1954–1975). The Lightning Bug was often used for **reconnaissance**. The drone hunted for enemies in the same way as an eagle or hawk. It had powerful cameras and could see enemies from high in the sky.

US forces also created long darts with giant sensors. The sensors acted like a bat's super sense of hearing. Soldiers threw the darts from aeroplanes. The darts landed in thick jungles and listened for enemies. Information about the enemy's location was then sent back to base.

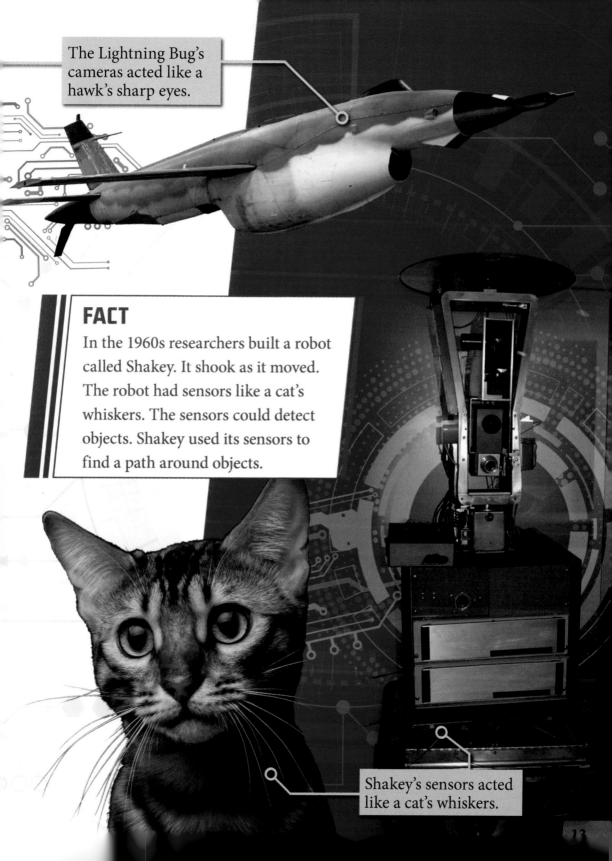

The Lightning Bug's cameras acted like a hawk's sharp eyes.

## FACT

In the 1960s researchers built a robot called Shakey. It shook as it moved. The robot had sensors like a cat's whiskers. The sensors could detect objects. Shakey used its sensors to find a path around objects.

Shakey's sensors acted like a cat's whiskers.

13

# Animal·inspired protectors

Modern machines often copy animal features too. Military robots and drones help to find enemies and disarm bombs. Some help in search and rescue missions. Just like animals, these machines come in all shapes and sizes.

Infrared and **ultraviolet** (UV) light are invisible to humans. Kestrels hunt prey using UV light. The RQ-11B Raven is a small UAV. It hunts out targets the way kestrels hunt for prey. But the Raven uses infrared light instead. It can find people in the dark.

A flower under UV light

kestrel

A soldier prepares to launch a RQ-11B Raven.

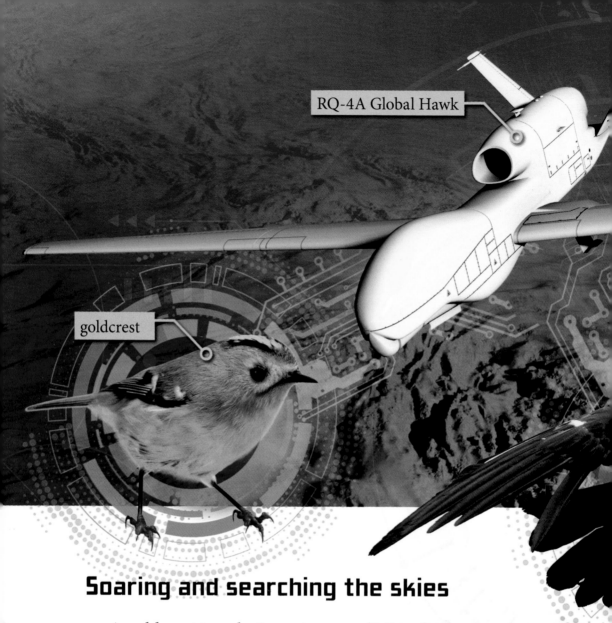

RQ-4A Global Hawk

goldcrest

## Soaring and searching the skies

A goldcrest is only 9 centimetres (3.5 inches) long. It's small, but it's a great flier. It can fly more than 480 km (300 miles) without stopping. Some UAVs also make long non-stop flights. The British Watchkeeper can fly for 16 hours straight. Its **radar**, camera and sensors gather information about enemy locations.

condor

The condor is a large bird that flies well in strong winds. It soars through the air with its wide wings. The RQ-4A Global Hawk performs **surveillance** missions. Like the condor, the Global Hawk is a strong flier. It can fly even in bad weather.

Lightweight SUGVs can be carried into action.

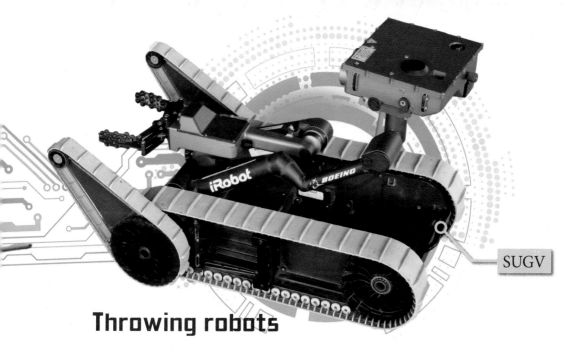

SUGV

## Throwing robots

Soldiers often need to make sure buildings are safe. To do so, they sometimes use Small Unmanned Ground Vehicles (SUGVs). They throw the 2.3-kilogram (5-pound) robots through windows. If one lands on its back, it can right itself like a cat. The robots have other cat-like features. They have cameras and sensors for great sight and hearing. They quietly search buildings for danger.

## Climbing, grabbing, lifting, smelling

The PackBot®, TALON, and Kobra™ are all similar robots. They travel over uneven ground with tracked wheels. They climb stairs as easily as mountain goats. The robots can also pick up objects. Their grippers work like the hands of monkeys and apes. The Kobra's™ arm can lift up to 150 kilograms (330 pounds).

TALON's gripper works like a monkey's hand.

These robots are often used to disarm bombs. They also perform dangerous search and rescue missions. They even imitate a dog's sense of smell. Their sensors can detect dangerous chemicals in the air.

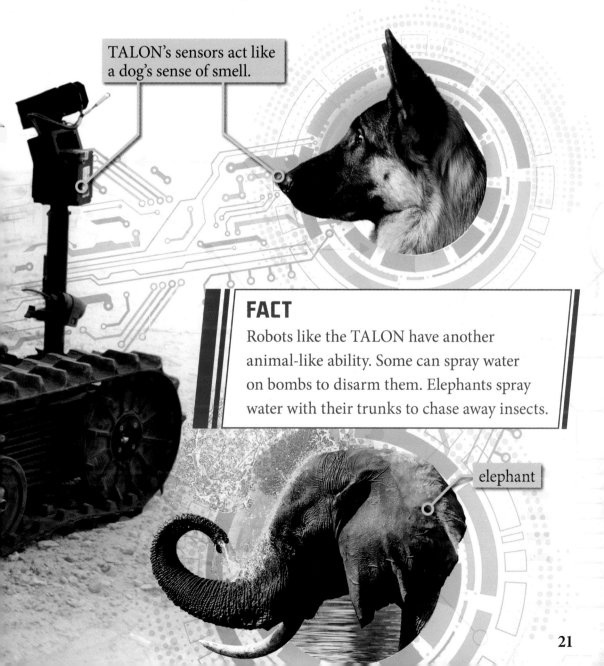

TALON's sensors act like a dog's sense of smell.

### FACT

Robots like the TALON have another animal-like ability. Some can spray water on bombs to disarm them. Elephants spray water with their trunks to chase away insects.

elephant

# Missions of the future

Inventors keep looking to nature to create new designs. The Ripsaw is a high-speed tank. Its tracked wheels work like a caterpillar's legs. The machine easily climbs steep hills. It smoothly rolls over obstacles. Armed forces hope to use the unmanned robot tank in future combat.

Ripsaw tank

RIPSAW-MS1

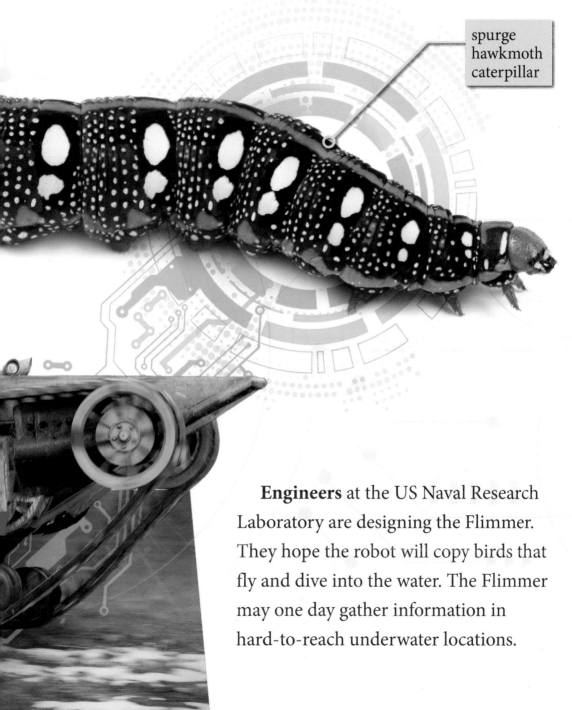

spurge
hawkmoth
caterpillar

**Engineers** at the US Naval Research
Laboratory are designing the Flimmer.
They hope the robot will copy birds that
fly and dive into the water. The Flimmer
may one day gather information in
hard-to-reach underwater locations.

Ground X-Vehicle wheels can change into a triangle shape.

## Flexible features

Inventors are also working on Ground X-Vehicles. These machines have wheels that can change shape based on the land. Some animals, such as the octopus, can also change themselves. They change their colour and shape based on their surroundings.

An octopus changes its colour and shape to hide among the rocks.

Researchers hope to create machines that change shape while flying. Inventors will have to study animals such as the northern white-faced owl. When facing a threat, the owl changes its shape to look more frightening.

The northern white-faced owl can change its shape to scare off enemies.

**FACT**

The V-Bat drone can fly straight up like a helicopter. Once in the air, it can soar like a bird. It flies well in windy weather. It can fly quietly for about eight hours.

The LS3 robot can carry heavy equipment over rough land like a horse.

## Copycats

Some robots look like the animals they are based on. The Legged Squad Support System (LS3) is like a robotic horse. It can carry about 180 kg (400 pounds) for 32 km (20 miles). These robots may one day help troops carry heavy gear across battlefields.

The Pleurobot looks like a salamander's skeleton. It's about the size of the Japanese giant salamander. It can walk over bumpy ground. It can also swim. The robot may one day help in search and rescue missions.

### FACT

Engineers are also designing robots that move like cockroaches. These small robots will have six moving legs and joints. They could help gather information, disarm bombs or find landmines.

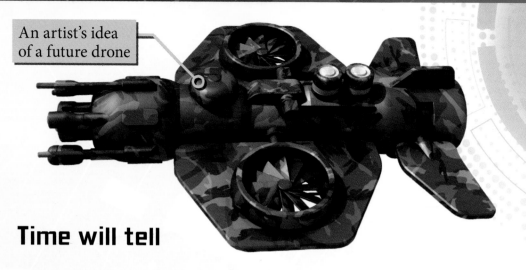

An artist's idea of a future drone

## Time will tell

Animals have developed unique features to survive in the wild. Inventors and engineers often study animals to build better machines. Studying animal abilities has led to many useful robots. Following nature's example, these machines can help to keep soldiers safe on future battlefields.

An artist's idea of a future robot

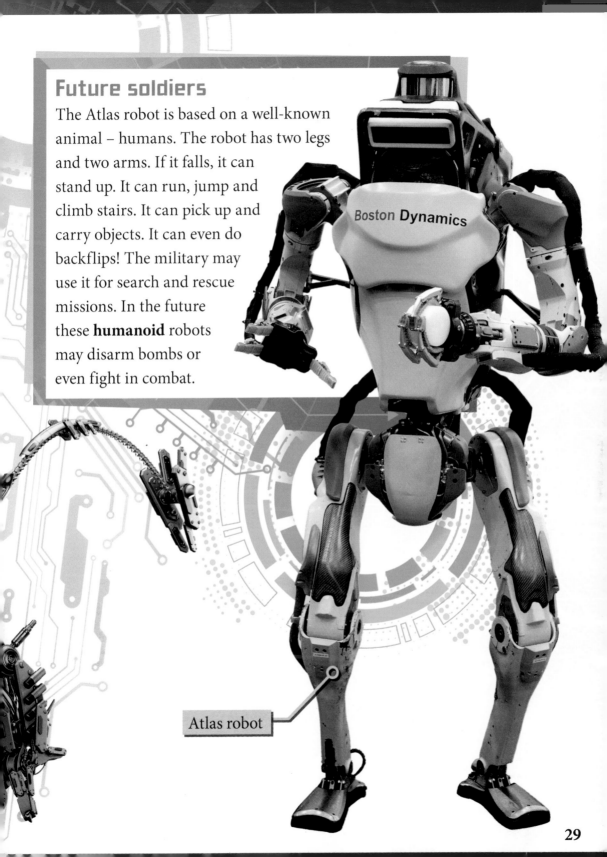

## Future soldiers

The Atlas robot is based on a well-known animal – humans. The robot has two legs and two arms. If it falls, it can stand up. It can run, jump and climb stairs. It can pick up and carry objects. It can even do backflips! The military may use it for search and rescue missions. In the future these **humanoid** robots may disarm bombs or even fight in combat.

Boston Dynamics

Atlas robot

# Glossary

**aerial** relating to something that happens in the air

**biomimicry** imitating the design of a living thing

**engineer** someone trained to design or build machines, vehicles, bridges and other structures

**humanoid** shaped somewhat like a human

**infrared** invisible waves of light that are usually given off by heat

**radar** device that uses radio waves to track the location of objects

**reconnaissance** gathering information about an enemy

**surveillance** keeping close watch on a person, place or thing

**terrorist** someone who uses violence and threats to frighten people

**torpedo** type of missile that usually travels underwater

**ultraviolet** invisible waves of light that can cause sunburn

# Find out more

## Books

*Animals* (DKfindout!), DK (DK Children, 2016)

*Animals That Hide* (Adapted to Survive), Angela Royston (Raintree, 2014)

*Incredible Robots in the Armed Forces* (Incredible Robots), Louise and Richard Spilsbury (Raintree, 2018)

*Military Drones* (Drones), Matt Chandler (Raintree, 2018)

## Websites

**www.dkfindout.com/uk/animals-and-nature**
Find out more about animals and their natural defences.

**www.dkfindout.com/uk/science/heat/heat-pictures**
Learn more about infrared light and thermal images.

# Index